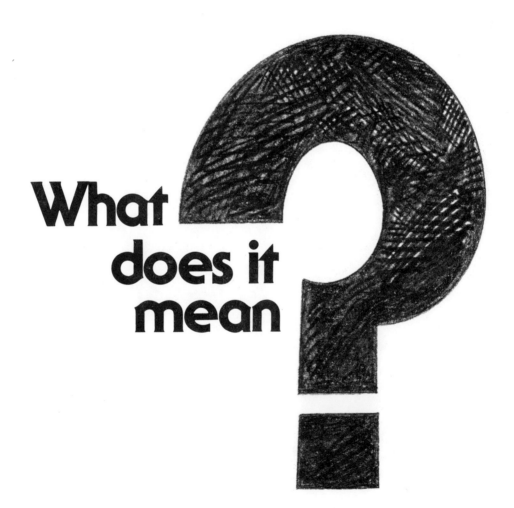

What does it mean?

What does it mean?

JEALOUS

by Sylvia Root Tester
illustrated by Nancy Inderieden

THE
CHILD'S
WORLD

ELGIN, ILLINOIS 60120

Library of Congress Cataloging in Publication Data

Tester, Sylvia Root.
  Jealous.

  (What does it mean?)
  SUMMARY: A child talks about how it feels to be
jealous and what can be done about it.
  1. Jealousy—Juvenile literature. 2. Sibling
rivalry—Juvenile literature. [1. Jealousy.
2. Babies]   I. Inderieden, Nancy.   II. Title.
BF575.J4T47   152.4   79-24042
ISBN 0-89565-111-4

Distributed by Childrens Press, 1224 West Van Buren Street, Chicago, Illinois 60607.

RR 1 2 3 4 5 6 7 8 9 10 11 12 R 91 90 89 88 87 86 85 84

I'm up in my room.
I've banged the door.

7

My face feels all
red. I'm kicking
the floor.
The trouble is this:
I'm jealous, you see.
Everyone here is
ignoring me.

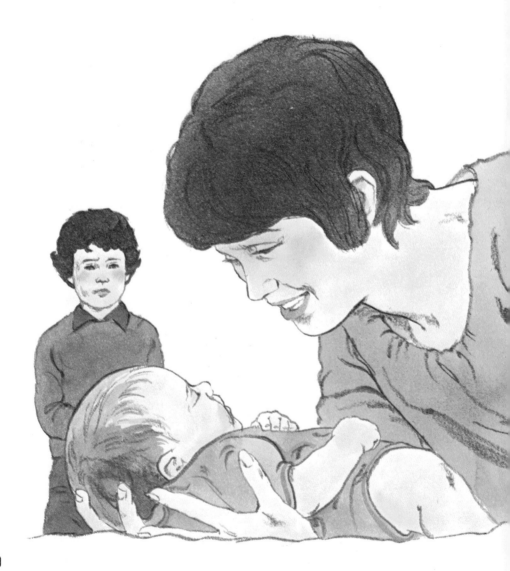

That baby's to blame!
Oh yes! He is!
Nothing's mine anymore!
All of it's his!

He's got my old room.
My little bed, too.
My mom's always loving
him, 'cause he's
so new.

13

Have you ever been

It doesn't feel right.
You want to kick
and scratch and bite.

I've been jealous
before! Oh, yes! Indeed!
I was jealous when
Betsy learned how
to bead,
and I couldn't do it.

17

But then I learned too.
I found out it wasn't
so hard to do.

I was jealous when Bill
got a brand new jet,

until I got busy
training my pet.

Here is Grandma,
knocking at my door.
She wants to see
the new rug on my floor...

23

and my big, new bed,
and the paint so white.

My dad did the painting.
He did it just right.

And Mom baked my
favorite cake last
night.

And Grandpa made me
a brand new kite.

29

I guess being jealous
isn't so smart.
There's still room for me
in everyone's heart.

Books in this series

Marks & Stanson
Cover
4/30/99 P. T.